Mrs. Clark,

Thanks again for all that you have done for me! I really cannot put into words my thanks. I truly believe that if it had not been for you, I would have not been able to _escape_ undergrad. I hope that you enjoy this work & that it blesses you more than it has me. Take care.

Katrina Franchot Jong

TSU C/o 1999

Still Waters

by

R. Franchot Long

Bloomington, IN  Milton Keynes, UK
authorHOUSE™

AuthorHouse™
1663 Liberty Drive, Suite 200
Bloomington, IN 47403
www.authorhouse.com
Phone: 1-800-839-8640

AuthorHouse™ UK Ltd.
500 Avebury Boulevard
Central Milton Keynes, MK9 2BE
www.authorhouse.co.uk
Phone: 08001974150

First published by AuthorHouse 7/18/2006

ISBN: 1-4259-2774-2 (sc)

Library of Congress Control Number: 2006903065

Printed in the United States of America
Bloomington, Indiana

This book is printed on acid-free paper.

Dedication:

For this dedication, I liken myself to a house,
and I want to thank those who helped me along the way,
those for making me who and what I am:

I thank Jesus Christ for being my foundation,
my family for being my wooden supports and trusses,
---structure and support is what I needed most,
my friends for being my doors and windows
---you let in the light and the fresh air,
the Saints for being my walls and roof,
---you help keep out the pests and the elements,
and my enemies, mockers, and doubters...
---for being the fertilizer for the trees around me,
making me look even better, helping me to stand against the winds,
and keeping me coolin' in the shade.

Table of Contents

Dreamy Waters

the Essence of Dreams Through Poetry

Dream Catcher

Everyone is made up of many different
people,
and some of us are of different animals too...
and all of these things
play a card in the hand of your success,
where the steaks are high; pass or fail,
and "I can't" is trying to outplay your hand.
...bluff you into believing in something
stupid.

Well for me,
I'm part insect...
and because of this part,
I get a chance to see many different things
in many different lights,
in many different ways,
all at the same time.

You see, I'm a Dream Catcher...
I can fly as high as the sky,
and move as quick as a thought.
Me and my four wings
can move and shake
with the best of 'em.
But because I'm so small,
I don't get shot at like the birds do,
or the planes...

My needs are simple.
All I need is a dream to catch...
I see it, I dive on it,
and I gobble it up before it knows what happened.
And then I move on to the next one.

A dream...a dream...that's all I need,
to keep this silvery-dragonfly lookin' body
of mine
movin' and groovin'.

Because I'm an insect,
I exist on a different plane...
people's "reality" just doesn't apply to me,
'cause they always using it as an excuse
as to why good things never come...
or to give them an excuse not to try...
or to chase after what they want...
Not me!
I'm going to chase all of my dreams,
and chase them so much
that failure is no longer an option.
All of my days will be sunny,
even when its pouring down rain.

So I'm going to take the different approach
to this,
and stay high above
where there are no windshields
for me to crash into,
where the warm air rises and stays,
and the view is always good.
I'm going to keep on glidin'
and ridin' along...
just buzzing to my own tune,
forever chasing and catching my dreams...

---Franchot

Floating...

Whispering on a cloud,
as I am a bird
that lights on a branch,
in the mighty oak of remembrance...

I float within the recesses of myself,
across memories
of people, places, and things,
past conversations
that move past my mind,
like ripples that emanate
from where the rock was thrown in the pond.
I'm floating...
I'm floating...

As my wings are full spread,
resting comfortably on the wind,
high in the sky am I,
as the sun begins to set
away in the distance...on the horizon.

Events go by, frame by frame,
and I remember
happy memories spent alone,
times spent with friends and family.
Times, like now,
spent inside myself,
floating upon my cloud...

Remembering...

---Franchot

Reflections…

Reflections in spirit,
reflections in time.
Thoughts impacting a reminiscing mind's eye
like the minute drops of rain,
sliding down the currents of the wind,
like children gliding down the chilled metal
of a sliding board,
---rain, hitting the pavement
in the smoothest of rhythms.

As I reflect upon past events,
my mind begins to move---
to places in the lands of yesterday,
of beautiful eyes seen from afar,
or easy conversations over coffee & candlelight.
To see your face again in my memories
continues to render my lungs useless
as you rob me of my breath again…

Reflections.
Of times past,
of times of favor and hardship.
Mirror images of experience…

---Franchot

Stylus

I'm sitting alone in the recesses
of my light-less apartment.
The record is spinning
& a dreamy mixture of moonlight and streetlight
comes gently through the blinds.
This soft light flies like a little dove
from the window
and lights on the stylus of my record player.
The soft metal dances upon the surface of the record
and glows like a shooting star,
traveling across the surface of a mountain lake.

As I stare,
that little stylus transforms,
in my mind's eye,
into a beautiful, young woman
dressed in pure white.
And as the slow tones of the love ballad
come forth from my speakers,
she begins to dance...
upon the shiny surface
of the vinyl.

Her body smoothly moving within the tides of the music,
to and fro,
ever so softly.
She traps me in the rhythm of her dance...
taking away the tired frustrations
of my hard day;
taking away the loneliness and pain
of everyday circumstances.
She is so soothing to watch,
so peaceful,
so serene.

And she stops dancing,
blows me a kiss,
and disappears with the same mystery
of her appearance.
The record has ended...

---Franchot

Parted Waters

Inspirations, Testimonies to the Greatness of Jesus Christ

As I Open My Heart to You

To be consumed by your awesome presence,
enveloped,
blanketed,
comforted by the soothing, serenity you bring to me,
it overcomes me like the quiet stillness of the countryside,
in the wee hours
of a starry morning.

Sitting quietly in my room,
as I can feel your presence about me,
filling my space—
my outer space & inner space—
with all of your fervent affections toward me,
your understanding,
your overwhelming passion...

And as I open up my heart to you,
to shower you with my affections,
my praises,
sprinklings of my ardent tempests,
—torrents of adoration towards you,
for you...
They are—my desperate attempts to bathe you in my love,
to dress you in the coat of my affections,
placing the banner of my being in love with you,
at your feet
and placing it tenderly around your neck.

And in this moment,
you grace me, share with me
your most intimate of thoughts,
your wisdom,
your understanding and guidance,
your love for no one but me...
bringing me to tears—with the goodness of You.

To sit upon your lap of love,
and to be encompassed by your magnificence,
your essence...
Just to sit and be bare before you,
without fault,
without contemplations of your possible contempt of me
for my infinitesimal wrongs and mistakes,
without shame,
without worry,
just without—
and have you love me because of who you are,
because you choose to,
despite all things.

Oh my love,
for I am unworthy of you,
but because of the very nature of you,
and because you want to, choose to,
because your love is all encompassing,
like the swells of the ocean during a typhoon,
it doesn't matter to you
what I've done wrong,
it doesn't matter how many times I've made mistakes between us,
the only thing that matters
is that you want me, and I want you...
regardless of all the details of life,
regardless of what's going on around in my circumstances,
for I worship you
because I have a need,
a burning,
panting,
aching need for you
growing within me...

Even though it will never be enough for me to say,
but I'll say it anyway,
I love you, Lord, with everything...

Brain Storming

Whispering dreams and melodies,
visions of love and enchanting seas,
floating like clouds over candlelight,
seeing a lover drifting silently out of my sight.
Life and existence are both for me
strange and intriguing, yet intangible mysteries,
with visions of the future looking so bright
and ambitions, needs, and wants all taking flight.

When the time comes,
where will you be?
Seen on the street, in between thighs, or drowned in
Hennessy?
When that trumpet sounds,
thunders really loud
and my Lord and brother Christ descends from the clouds.
And the world gets ready for the belt,
the beating of no end,
and to the stars, into heaven we will ascend.
When the devil has his day that is all night
and grips the world in his clutches, holding them all with
fingers of fright.

Pleasures and joy,
laughter to no end
life made of clouds with silver linings, His to lend
and peace & respect,
no worries or fights
and I will be floating
like the clouds over candlelight.

---Franchot

Can't Get in Touch with Your Heart

To see you
as often as I do,
sitting, waiting, watching...
for you to see me
and look upon me with the adoration
that is a reflection of all that I feel for you...

To see you each time,
walking,
breathing,
talking,
-each activity is a piece of an awesome ballet,
symphony,
orchestration of the most velvety of prose,
smooth, pristine in every essence
like silk that flows over the edge of the falls,
as a smooth, intoxicating, fragrant liquid
that flows over the frost
that hangs from a mountain pine
upon the side of a snowy hill.
I am immersed
in a warm, soothing bubble bath
of adoration towards you.
If you would only see me,
give me access to your heart,
that I might treasure it for all of my days...

As you look upon her,
I look upon you,
with a love and adoration
that is quite the same...
For I am the river source
of all the hypnotic, silken feelings

that the light of your heart
shines upon her.
But, I wish that you would direct that light
upon me...
For you to look upon my face,
and see your own true image,
to long to be held within the safe confines of my arms
to be bounced upon my knee,
for I am your eternal Father,
who stares endlessly
at the horizons of your heart,
longing to see your smiling face
as you come into view,
while you make your journey towards me.
For she is not totally your home,
only a shining part of it.
I am the structure inside which
your home is built.
I long to give her to you,
but my heart cries, pleads
for you to give your heart to me.
For I can do things with and in you
that she cannot even fathom.
I wish to be the lover of your soul
because I'll never stop loving you...
Unconditionally...

I won't become angry with you,
only to cut off my love,
I am above your ways and thoughts,
I am the answer that you seek
within the quiet recesses of your heart,
oh my precious possession,
I long for you...
I gave everything to be apart of you,
my child,
my effort,

my protection and time,
all for you.
I never say anything to you
because of the heat of the moment,
won't go back on any promises made,
for I am holy and righteous,
and I will hold and protect your heart
if you would only give it to me to have,
and believe in me...
As I watch you as you watch her...
for like you,
I can't quite get in touch with my beloved's heart...

---Franchot

I Haven't the Right
(*inspired by "The Passion of the Christ"*)

I haven't the right...
to complain,
for You took lashes that I could not take,
peels, cuts, rakes...
strung like a human side of beef
meat for the slaughter,
all because of your mission
to save me, to save us
from sin...
All because—you had a mission of love.

I haven't the right...
to be upset with others
who think differently than I..
For You were beaten like a criminal,
tied up like some crazed animal,
bled, gutted—like a fish on a block,
all for me & my wretched kind
to fulfill prophesy foretold,
all for the writing of lyrics
for your love ballad to the FATHER
on our behalf:
"Forgive them, for they not know what they do."

I haven't the right...
to be defiant of you.
Holding true to what my feeble, little mind
thinks it can comprehend
without having the infinite wisdom
of You
or without having the eyes that can dare to see
the severity—
of the entirely dark,

decrepit,
desperately wicked playing field
that is
the hearts and minds of men.
I have not the right...
Without the ability to see
the whole black & white checked board
of life.

I haven't the right...
to be arrogant.
Filled only with myself
and what I think is right
coupled with unbalanced concern for myself and no other,
based not on what You have said,
but based on that which I think that I know.
Knowledge that only came
by the grace of your hand,
not by my ability to absorb
not by my being so privileged
but because of your insight, sight in—
to my lack of wisdom
and by your wink
that made it so,
in my mind.
I haven't the right...

An epic battle won that day...
without the drawing of a sword,
the cock of a rifle's hammer,
without the wisping of the leather
of a slingshot...
but by the lifting of a tree,
by the cuts across your flesh,
the stripes through which I am healed...
A battle won in purposeful silence.

With wood and nails,
you built more that day
than any of my years at a time,
ever could
with steel and construction crews in my hands.

I have *not* the right
—but because of you King Jesus,
and what you did
out of selfless love for me,
I can stand.

---Franchot

The Awakening

I was awakened after...

fallin' through the pitch blak chasm,
endless limits of falling space,
walls riddled with shards of glass,
jagged pieces
of broken esteems,
broken hearts,
broken dreams.
Wounded every second from slidin'
down the sharp pieces
at ludicrous speeds.
Gnashing of teeth
as the tears in my eyes burned
like pain dressed in a hockey mask
lookin' fo' every opportunity
to yank my flesh on some more glass,
as I was falling,
falling,
falling,
swallowed whole by a darkness
that deepened as I fell.

Broken times,
amazing frustrations,
fits of <u>rage</u>,
fragmented relationships...
jagged glass on a wall I can't see
slicing me
as I bump and slam around,
twisting and turning,
churning every which way the *devil wishes*,

in the midst of my great fall
falling,
falling—
fallen...nature.

None of this makes sense!
countless,
ceaseless,
bitter,
agony...
I didn't ask for a life like this!
I didn't ask for a life,
so why is my world so dark,
with all of this glass,
bleeding from my arms,
my heart,
my soul,
bleeding...
clear blood from my eyes
—tears
...with each day
as I'm falling,
before the Awakening,
falling on rocks,
stones,
falling uncontrollably
gnashing,
ripping, tearing in pitch blakness
as I fall further
and further in.

Bullets fly forth,
slamming through the flesh of my sanity,
agony,
as she laughs and points,
as he threatens,
as she yells,

as they are unfair to me and to mine,
as our pockets have holes,
as the bill is left unpaid,
as the lights are turned off,
as loneliness cuts
like someone stabbing me with a spoon,
as the world spins,
and life spits in my face,
falling,
falling...
—fallen...nature,
as the evil one laughs at me hysterically...

Then in the midst of my fall,
a hand reached out from the darkness,
reached out from the wall
of my fallen space,
and stopped me dead in the air.
A lifeless me,
a broken me,
a shattered reflection
of a mirror of a boy...

And slowly the hand of PURE holiness,
cut through the darkness,
flippin' on the switch,
setting my falling space ablaze with light!
And a lifeless, bruised, tired, weeping me
began to rise,
and rise,
and grow,
and heal,
and rise.
The hand rubbed my eyes
and I began to see,
as I heard the angry howl of the enemy
laying a pitiful, angry claim
to something that was *no longer* his plaything.

As I was Awakened,
I rose,
and rose,
and life *became* a crystal stair,
until I shot forth from the mouth of the pit,
that I had been birthed in,
and I saw the one whose hand it was,
in all of His brilliant white,
with hair of wool and skin of bronze,
and a crown of light upon his head.
I was Awakened...
as that hand
pulled me forth into its arm,
and I was covered by His other arm
as I was embraced...
loved eternally.
...I was awakened.

---Franchot

The Blood...pt. 1

Dirty, filthy, horrid in my sin,
stinking, rank
decrepit from within,
rotting, deplorable
stank from end to end,
without a hope or clue
damnation's my fin...

Running, racing
through the pages of my life,
lying, manipulating,
rage, fear, and strife.
Going through my years
without any light,
broken and hurting
not knowing I was stife-
ling-all these things
were contained within,
darkness and chaos
were all that dwelt herein,
within...inside-out
of my heart of sin
the battle for my soul
I could not win.

Call me, He did
in His small, still voice,
"No!" I replied,
"I still have a choice!"
And I ran to do it *my* way
and lived life without rejoice,
but love pulled me up
& out with a hoist.

His blood surrounded me,
there was nowhere I could go,
it streamed along and jumped on me
replacing my dirt with snow.
Clean and pure my heart became
---within, His light did glow.
Why He saved a wretch like me
my mind will never know.

Looking back,
being whole now,
I can see that I was attacked,
in a war to which the awareness of
the world is taking a nap.
Accept His blood! Accept His blood!
Please! before He comes back
to take His church home, us alone,
for the rest will burn in Evil's trap.

---Franchot

Reflective Waters

Rippling Images/Expressions
of Life and Memories

A Glance of an Angel

A single touch from your hand
as you pass by me through the door of the store. . .
A glance into your sparkling brown eyes. . .
a smile that lightens your face,
and brightens my world,
erupts into the melodic chimes
that only my heart can hear.
With just a single glimpse,
I am forever enchanted by your beauty,
and my life---
will be eternally marked,
forever covered in a velvety rapture
held willingly captive
by continuous thoughts of you.
Wondrous intoxication
that quickens my pulse
as my eyes yearn to caress more of you with my gaze,
as an unquenchable desire to speak to you
roars within my soul. . .
But you, my angel
have disappeared from view
from behind the sliding glass doors,
and I walk on,
embracing a love
that will never bloom.

---Franchot

Alone

It feels funny to be alone...
you never quite understand how it happens.
Your friends seem to all fly away,
like the seeds of the dandelion...
dancing upon the swift currents
of the carefree wind.

Everyone and everything
seem so far away...
like a dream that can be seen, yet never realized--
elusive.

The sun shines upon your back
and your shadow is not there to walk you along.
It, like everyone else
has something better to do.
Your heart cries,
your eyes begin to tear,
and your pride melts away
like an icicle in a child's hand...
piece by piece,
drop by drop.

Being alone—
like the bitter sting
of being stabbed with a spoon...

---Franchot

The Age of Innocence

It's very funny
that the young wish to be old,
and that the old wish to be young.
Why can't we, just simply be
what we are?

It's been said that being young is a wonderful thing,
and this is so.
This is the time when the heart is light,
the imagination is vast,
and the spirit is rich.
The eyes see no color
the ears hear no pain.
The hands and mouth can do no wrong.
The world is filled with the gentleness of the sweetest music.
Rapture of laughter and the joys of play.
Time is meaningless,
goes on without bound.
The air is sweet and the times are good.
This is the beauty of being young;
the essence of childhood.

As the young become the old,
the world becomes a dark and sinister place.
The bright sunny days
have all turned to storm clouds and rain.
The freedoms of life have all been confined
by the chains of responsibility.
The heart becomes heavy,
laden down with pain and worry over an uncertain future.
The imagination, says society,
is childish and useless.
The spirit becomes tired.

The eyes now see color,
conflicting shades of black and white.
The ears hear the screams of the world's pain.
The hands and mouth commit the deadliest of sins.
The world is filled with corruption.
And life develops a scowl, rather than a smile.

Things would be better if we all learned
to be like the child we all once were.
To learn to see the good in everything.
To learn to forgive the unforgivable.
To love all.

It's funny how we all waste our childhoods
trying to be like the old.
Let's not waste our adulthood,
let's help the world and ourselves
by trying, in so many ways, to act
like the children.

---Franchot

The BLAKNESS or the Darkness (Which is Which?)

As I look around at this world,
and see the times and circumstances
in which we live,
the image clearly appears in my mind
that my people are living in the dark ages...
They've had *their* dark ages centuries ago,
but we transverse the desolation of our desert
now...
in the ironic age of *enlightenment*.

Looking around
and all I see are Black faces of doom,
of regret,
of anguish...
shattered dreams
and broken hearts,
heads without knowledge to fill them up
or a care or a hope
to kindle the spirit's flame.

We shut off our love from one another,
placing the entire race in a room without light,
without doors or windows.
And in this room we clash and battle.
None of us knows what we are fighting each other for
and no one knows who anyone else is...
but in the darkness,
it doesn't matter
because just like in the Blakness,
we are all the same.

Everyday we all wear a mask
that is just like that dark room:

it hides what we truly think,
what we truly feel,
who we truly are.
And we wear this mask willingly.
But our mask, like our Blakness and/or darkness
keeps us from soaring with the birds,
and dancing on the golden drops of the sun's rays
and prevents us from ascending into the starry heavens
—to the places where we should be,
but we're still stuck in this bucket,
putting claws to the legs of the one
who is strong enough to make it to the rim...

We have no more family,
we have no history,
we have no love
because we wear the mask of darkness
or are captured in that blak room
—we deny all of these things.
Our children have no respect,
our women try to be men,
our men try to be spineless,
your brother is no longer your keeper
but a diabolical enemy
dressed up in the Trojan horse of "being down",
and peace and respect
have been cut away;
money, cars, and bling-bling
are our new family values.
And we wonder why we don't prosper,
we wonder why we cannot find love,
and we have the audacity
to wonder why the milk of human kindness
has been turned into a cup
of warm piss...

Is our Blackness blakness or darkness?

---Franchot

Encouragement

I know what it's like
being trapped in lightless room with no doors,
just you and your problems,
sitting there…staring at one another,
with nothing but space and opportunity between you.
And then they come at you…
the only trick to this nightmarish scenario
is that its jet-black darkness all around
and they can see you,
but all you see is blackness.

Yeah,
I've been in situations like that,
trapped in this room called frustration,
and all you know
is that you want out…and out now.
The ones who put you in there,
whether it be someone else
or even you,
have set the stage
and you must play it out…
scene by scene.

But always remember,
that God doesn't close a door
without opening a window,
and that all things work for the good of His children,
---that one day,
this room is going to develop some light that you can use
and you'll be able to fight effectively,
properly,
victoriously.
'Cause God will have a flashlight to appear in your hand
and will cause you to win out.

Stay encouraged…

---Franchot

Chestnuts

They say
that the power of a beautiful woman's glance
is strong enough to slow down time,
awesome enough to make the world stop spinning,
at least for an instant...

And when I was walking by
and your glance shook hands with mine,
my world,
this life's existence—
slowed down.
Every sound tiptoed slowly across my ears,
like a child coming past his napping mother
on the way to the cookie jar,
and the people throughout the room,
moving in slow motion,
were placed gently within the wooden chest
of unimportance,
locked away...
and all I could do
was focus on your precious
chestnut brown eyes.

Captivating, beautiful eyes,
the windows to the soul.
Pretty enough to tell a story in vivid imaginations,
with awe-striking elegance
that is a visual melody
to a symphony of dreamy, hypnotic expressions.
All brought forth through God's admiration
for his daughter's beauty
...making her the keeper,
the recipient,

of such an awesome and wonderful gift,
the wearer of the stunning gown of a beautiful face
to the grand, exquisite ball that is your life,
accented by those striking,
enchanting,
chestnut brown eyes
of yours...

---Franchot

I'm Builidin' Me a Home

Have pride in yourself
my son,
for all that is in this great land,
a part of you has helped build.
From the stoplights in the streets to the refrigerators at home,
from the city layout of Washington, DC to the cellular phone,
the parts of you
that come from generations past
have born great achievements
despite the hissing, gnashing nine heads
of adversity.

We have traveled a long way on our journey,
climbing that crystal stair…
But with each step
we continue on,
marching past Jim Crowe,
past the glass ceiling,
and past the statistics and the media hype,
that cast that dark shadow of stereotype over our heads,
all the way up towards the roof…
that place of economic and social empowerment,
a place of equality,
where the air will be fresh and sweet.

Be proud of your home,
my son
for each brick within its sacred walls
has been created from the blood, sweat, tears, and pain
of those pillars of strength,
who not only advanced themselves,
but bore on their crosses
the responsibility of catapulting generations.

For every part of the roof of your home has been forged
through the agony, frustration, and perseverance
of Harriet Tubman, Joseph Cinque, and John Brown…
Each floorboard was laid through the efforts
of Asa Phillip Randolph, Ida B. Wells, Dred Scott…
Each door and window was perfectly put into place
through the ingenuity and talents
of Elijah McCoy, Louis Lattimer, Daniel Hale Williams…
 Each part of its foundation
was laid by the awesome strength of character
of Booker T. Washington, Fredrick Douglas, Josephine Baker…
Zora Neil Hurston, Lorraine Hansberry, Langston Hughes…

Be proud, my son
be proud!
For your home's foundation's is solid
and your roots run deep.
Raise your head high,
for the strength that brought you forth
from those of your ancestry,
will sustain you
and will help you to build the skyscraper
for yourself
and for those yet to come.

---Franchot

Waters of Eros~~~

the Warm, Tender Depths
of the Romantic Deep

A Beating Heart...

Rolling over slowly next to my darling wife,
so close
that I ended up, somehow, in her arms...
And as I sat there listening to her tender heart beat,
it put me peacefully back asleep
like a sweet lullaby,
brought forth from her lips
to float gracefully upon my ears.

And during my peaceful plummet,
I began to feel the loving embrace
of my lover's beating heart,
as it whispered "I adore you",
in a gentle, rhythmic embrace
full of sweet caresses,
downy kisses,
and bursting with fondant affections.

And I had pleasant dreams that night...
of she,
my angel.

---Franchot

A Sketch

And as the droplets of dew
slowly settle upon the sea of grasses,
As they gently dance along with the currents of the wind,
and the first rays of the brand new dawn
gently melt through the surface of the horizon
and trickle onto the day,
I hear the presence of singing...

I hear the sweet, subtle songs of the birds,
as they glide gently into the brand new skies far above.
And as the soft lullabies of the pines & evergreens
when they allow the winds
to race through their fingers...
I am remembering a sweet memory of you...

---Franchot

A Whisper in Moonlight

Patient...
quietly watching your essence
across the room,
seeing your hair,
as it flows down your back like Niagra,
seeing and caressing every inch of your angelic form...
You look so soft and delicate to me,
so darling in that soft touch...
that caress of the light of the moon.

As I hold you,
you melt my fears,
you nourish my soul,
you stir all of the love
that beats in my heart and through my veins,
keeping me alive with just a whisper of your love,
it nourishes me
in ways that I can only dream about describing.
—I am captivated by you.

And as I hold you close to me,
I cherish...
every inch of you
and whisper to you sweetly,
a proposal,
in the down brightness of the moon...
"Forever be mine."

---Franchot

An Untitled Poem of Love

From beyond the sunset,
beyond the gates of time,
past the gates of memory...
I look in the mirror
And I see you eyes staring lovingly into mine.

I cannot see the rest of your face
as my heart begins to burn
with the embers of passion
set afire by rays of light
rocketing forth through the endless skies
as they light my world,
from your angelic face.

My yearn for you,
my need for you,
to have you fill my lungs
and entice my soul,
to touch you,
as my fingers trace the surface of the glass
as your hands match mine in the reflection.
And as my eyes begin to tear
from being denied a touch of your essence,
I see that you are crying also,
that your eyes are replaced with my own.
And I begin to smile
as I realize that my reflection
is of you, and you of me
...because we are one and the same,
my love.

---Franchot

Being in Love...

When two are in love...
all those around can see its glow.
No one needs to utter a word,
no glances need to be exchanged,
just that light that shines from above
that they reflect off of their hearts
onto one another.

Love...complicated simplicity:

Euphoric whirlwind that tornadoes
around your heart around a room
like a hurricane,
spinning an' dippin' and risin'
and feeling light as a feather in a brook
that flows through the sky,
just you and yo' love bird
through the endless reaches of space & time,
running through each rain drop that falls,
sliding down on the rainbows like children
into each other's arms,
each other's smiles,
each other's eyes,
into the wonderful bliss
while being stowaways on a wonderful ride
through the light that encompasses the world
in gold
whenever your special someone enters yo' space...

Just the two of them...
that's all they need to exist,
one cleaving to another,
one can be the heart

while the other is the lungs,
pumping—
the bubbly, silky bath
of endorphins,
the quiet, beautiful land where they live & love
to be carried into the waiting arms of matrimony,
where they will abide under the shadow of the Almighty,
and He nods and says:
"Now that's good..."

---Franchot

Caress

Waking to a beautiful essence,
with the touch of the sunlight
as it caresses the smoothness
of your skin.

As I touch you tenderly
with my fingertips...
With each stroke,
I fall in love with you all over again.
And as I touch the melodies
within your now slumbering eyes
with my heart,
as I feel your heart beat
whilst I hold you,
clutching you as if you were my last breath,
my love for thee deepens
and causes tears to swell
in my eyes,
when I look at you.

I love you, my treasure,
and I'm falling deeper and deeper within
as I continue to look upon you
...and caress you ever so delicately,
with the tenderness of my heart...

---Franchot

Completion
(a poetic conversation between two who are in love)

He to she...

Ecstatic happiness when I look at you,
to melt into your arms at the slightest touch,
music is what I hear whenever you are near,
my precious,
—the chimes of my heart
play the melodies of our song,
as I peer...captivated, into your eyes.

Her reply...

Your touch,
your essence,
the completing power that you have to satisfy my soul,
with each loving glance that you give,
you quench the thirst
of the core of my being....
I love you with everything.

The response to his beloved...

Whenever your caressing gaze
comes to greet the look of love in my eyes,
my heart quivers
—as the gentle snowflake of affectionate rhapsodies
melts into every fiber of my mind
and sets off shockwaves,
like that felt by a rose of scarlet
as it is embraced
by a gentle kiss in a spring breeze.

The lady's reply to her love...

I rejoice whenever you come close to me,
for I am that which hath come from my Adam's side,
to be nurtured and protected
within the wondrous blossoms
of our garden,
eternally grateful to the Father,
who created you carefully, fearfully, wonderfully...
just for me
to love& cherish,
help and complete.
I will always be blessed,
for we are the two parts of a ring,
not two halves, but one continuous whole
—forever complete
within each other's love...

---Franchot

Embers & Lights

With just a single gaze upon your face
my love,
a melody is produced from the core of my soul
filling the air
and surrounding us in a fondant atmosphere
of the splendor of our love.
Each time that we stare into each other's eyes,
those abysses of our very being,
we descend ever so sweetly again,
and again—
helplessly,
willingly,
drowning in the warm, soothing elixir
of our beating heart
—just you and I
together.

With just a single touch from you,
my twin soul,
the wells of my eyes fill
with the tears that only the splendor of joy can bring,
a joy of a dream come true,
that of adoring you for the rest of my years,
watching each other turn silver,
counting everyday—the steps to your heart,
embracing and dressing you tenderly
in amour
as we fly into the warm, peaceful raptures of our passion
while the magnetic Eros between us
bursts into a symphony of lights
that fall to earth like tears from the heavens.

To you,
my sweetest love,
the one who completes me ever so tenderly,
I can say that I'm truly blessed
for having you as my heartfelt companion,
a fellow explorer upon our life's journey.
With each thought of you,
the embers of my heart are doused
with the most potent of fuels,
erupting into an inferno of fervor
that blazes through me,
reflects throughout you,
and gently,
romantically,
warms us
as we embrace each other
and whisper "I do"
again and again
lovingly, in each other's ear...

---Franchot

Gateway to Matrimony

I look behind
to gaze upon you,
you are glowing, floating in your white gown,
like an angel softly gliding across a sunbeam of light,
into my arms.

As I stare helplessly captivated,
enchanted,
mesmerized by your hypnotic beauty,
by the intoxicating soft browns of your eyes
through that cloudlike veil
that crowns your beautiful, flowing hair.
You gracefully make your way down the aisle
to my awaiting arms
that are thirsting for an embrace of you.
And when your father releases you
into my humble care,
I stare into your eyes lovingly,
drawing my very breath from your unending love for me,
the very love that sustains me,
the other half
of that
which sustains us.

As I look at you, and you at me...
And I see that sparkle in your eyes,
that very shimmering, glimmering light
that tells me within my spirit
that you belong to me to you.
And as we stand together
before that gateway of matrimony,
of togetherness,
of oneness,

you take my hand in yours,
and my heart begins to cry tears of quickened joy
because our love is becoming an institution...

And as I stare into that veil and see your soul,
my fiancé,
as you slowly emerge from your angelic-white cocoon,
that which is transforming you into my wife
before my very eyes,
to be placed gingerly into my side as my missing rib,
my pulse quickens,
and my eyes tear,
as they are blinded by your beauty...
Your eyes tear from behind the veil,
expressing your overwhelming love and joy...
and I lace my fingers into yours
as the pastor continues his wonderful words...
I hold onto you as though you were my last breath.
And I stare lovingly into your eyes into mine,
and I look at how...
how handsome you are my groom,
standing tall in your tux,
as though it were a shining suit of silver armor,
as you, my knight, stand before me,
promising to protect me from all harm,
promising to cover me,
provide for me,
fulfilling your role ordained by the Lord himself,
as I pledge my heart,
myself,
my love
to you on this blessed day.
Your looking lovingly at me
sets me afire with raging blue flames of amour,
as you slowly emerge from that awesome beam of white light,
that has shot forth from the heavens
to consume my fiancé

and dissipate
like a fog in the soft rays of an early morning,
revealing my husband,
in all of his handsome splendor,
the king of my love,
my heart's true desire in all of his magnificence.

And as your vows to me emerge joyously from your lips,
and mine audibly sprout wings all their own
and take flight,
you place your ring upon my third finger,
symbolic of the trinity of our marriage:
the Lord, you, & I,
and as I place my ring upon your finger,
we stare ahead
as the gateway to Holy oneness is opened,
and we walk through together.
As you take me softly into your arms,
and my eyes tear even more,
as do yours,
you kiss me kiss you kissing us, we kiss
as we seal the door on ourselves
as we are now one...
forever.

---Franchot

Oneness

When I look upon you, my love,
I see all that completes me.
Caressing you, my most precious,
with my most tender of gazes,
I see you move,
watch you talk,
observe the secrets of your soul
contained neatly within the locket of your heart...
And I am captivated,
beyond the reach of any and all words,
beyond the stretches of the most vivid of imaginations,
and can only communicate the potency
of the way I feel for U, to U,
is through my love.
It is the only gateway through which I can convey
the rich expanses
of the awesome depths of everything that lies within me,
all for you.

When I think of you & I
and all of the experiences that we've shared together,
the spectrum of gentle emotions within me begin to swell
and erupt like a towering volcano,
whose hot lava spews from my eyes
as velvety tears down my cheeks
whenever I look upon you,
my air,
and I fall in love with you
...all over again.

And when my sweet dreams of us
require more detail,
I reflect on how the oneness we share
reminds me of the first union in Eden's Garden,
perfectly wonderful and complete.
Complicated simplicity,
a creamy mixture of silken roughness
and candied amour,
the oneness between us, within us
rages like a massive inferno of blue flame,
the hottest of all the flames,
and yet is so tender…
that it, like a babe in swaddling,
needs to be fed by our love for one another
and tended to,
to be kept vibrant and whole.

So come with me, my beloved,
and let us tend our flame,
here in Eden's Garden,
and be sustained by our love,
while our souls are quickened with true oneness,
'til death do us part…

---Franchot

Smitten

The very essence,
the want of you and your presence,
to inhale the velvety rhapsodies
of the scent of your hair,
as my fingertips thirst
for another touch of your hand,
a caress across your arms...
to hold you with such—care...
such love...
Oh, I'm smitten with you...

To look upon your pristine form,
to embrace the vivid enchantment
of your intoxicating smile,
to caress you with my most shy of gazes,
laying my eyes gently upon you
creates a hypnotic euphoria
that covers my heart completely,
like the rhythmic wave of lights of the Aurora,
with colour & light,
as it covers the stretches—
of the northern skies.

My heart pants at the thought of you,
my very being cries out to see you again,
and again,
and *again*...
until my most passionate of desires
becomes enveloped
—into the most romantic eruptions,
a burning flame

consuming my every thought
—whose numbers match
the flaps of a humming bird's wings
in slow motion flight.
Oh dearest...I'm smitten...

Just a hint that you'll be coming to me,
my heart clicks its heels
and takes flight upon the outstretched wings of amour,
flying to heights
only touched by the angels of heaven...
gliding upon sunbeams
that rocket forth from the horizons
upon vivid reds, pinks, oranges, & yellows—
Colours that melt gingerly into the skies,
and descend to earth like the minute drops of *raine*,
each tender drop...
falling into the palm of your downy, precious hand...
My beloved—
smitten am I with you.

Your name is like a romantic andante,
wrapped carefully within the notes and lyrics of a love ballad,
like a babe in a downy, silken blanket,
tickling my ears whenever it passes my lips.
And when I embrace you my beloved,
my most precious treasure,
and have you look up into my eyes
with your flawless, tender, loving innocence,
and I hear the light whisper of "Baby...I love you so..."
as it pours from your lips
like honey over the spout of a pitcher
onto my ears and into my heart,
the strings of amour within my soul
begin to play softly
and passionately to you,
as our love melts into each others' very being

like a snowflake upon a window sill in December,
as our lips meet slowly & sweetly...
as we are fervently—

...smitten.

---Franchot

Soul Dancin'

The way your eyes look,
in the light of the coming dawn.
The way your lips smile,
when you're feelin' what I'm feelin'.
The way your gentle hands glide over mine,
underneath the fleeting stars,
forever riding with the night.
And then I kiss you...

When our lips meet,
our souls begin to dance,
outside of us,
within us,
surrounding us.
Set to the music and tempo
of the ending night,
and the sweet melody of the coming dawn.
Our love makes us dance,
our love makes us rise,
like the awakening birds
who take flight from the dewy grasses.
And like the light that begins to peak over the horizon,
you light my life,
you warm my heart,
and you give me the ability
to see my world,
our world,
as we dance.

---Franchot

Untitled Love

An extension of my arms,
the keeper of my heart,
my strength when I am without,
my precious one,
the one that I love.

With every pulse of my heart,
I draw nearer to you,
my soul cries to be closer to you,
to feel the kiss in your smile,
the gentleness in your spirit,
the dance in the way that you say hello.

With the very gaze of you,
I feel my body quicken,
the love that I feel for you cannot be contained,
and it overflows and explodes
all over you,
encompassing us in warm, tranquil liquids,
like that of a bubble bath,
or liquid sunshine on a frosty, winter day.
To the one I love,
the one I hold—
to keep and cherish with every breath,
every smile,
every...

thing.

---Franchot

A Vow
(a promise from my heart)

The altar is full of candles,
and the organ begins to release the timeless chimes
of the march across love's golden pastures.
And through the crowd of onlookers,
sitting on opposite sides of the church,
I see your beautiful, angelic form
gracefully floating down that aisle...
coming to me like a precious dove
flying through the air,
coming gently, to lite on one of my branches
and create a cozy little nest
within the quiet recesses of my heart.

As we take our places at each other's side,
I look slowly over to you for assurance,
for strength,
for someone, that special someone—
you,
to share in my thought.
Baby, please read my mind...

I see your smile through that pristine vale,
like the sun that shines on me through the clouds
to remind me that everything is going to be alright.
And as I look into your precious eyes,
I see your awesome love for me,
and I see that this moment was meant to happen,
from the day that I came into being,
when God made me from the dust
blown by the four winds,
and just before he planted me

on this beautiful Earth
he took from me, my rib
and upon his great workbench he created
his finest work,
his grandest piece of art,
the extra that makes me extraordinary...
you.
He created you for me for you.

And when he planted me here,
he made it
 so that Cupid, with his subtle ammunition,
would help me to find you,
and here I am
about to be reunited with my long, lost rib
like a key and a lock that are joined
to open the gates of love,
the gates of heaven on Earth,
the gates to this alter
to enter the enchanted lands of matrimony,
forever by your side...
And for such a chance, this great opportunity,
such a precious gift as you
to be given to me unconditionally,
I vow before everyone here,
before the Almighty and all of his angels,
to be at one with you always,
to be beside you,
to protect you,
to try to be understanding
despite all circumstances and situations,
to hold you in my heart and arms forever,
to be supportive of you,
to listen (even though I will argue),
but most important of all,
to place you within me,
to fit you back into my body,

into my soul, and into my heart
and love you as hard
and as true as I can,
for as long as I shall draw breath...

---Franchot

When I Look at You

In the early dew of the morning,
as the Sun rises
from beneath his bedtime blanket of the horizon,
and as his first few rays
dance upon the blinds of our window,
I awake and roll over gently
to caress my precious wife with my loving gaze.

And as my eyes stare and feast upon her angelic beauty,
I am rendered speechless
by the melodic chimes___the beating of her tender heart,
by her sleeping innocence,
like a child playing in the rain,
and by her natural splendor,
proof of God's awesome palette and brushes...
those who created her.

Then she gently wakes to see the satiny tear of thanksgiving
that glides down my cheek...
And she gently whispers: "I love you too, my dearest."

---Franchot

Rain Storm Waters

Tear drops Streaming Down the Sides of a Sorrowful Heart

A Candle in the Rain

I was flying through the hills
and stopped and landed
in a mighty oak
to rest and stretch my wings.
Oddly enough,
I saw a group of humans below...

I had never seen anything like this before.
The spirit that I had witnessed,
was so moving,
so powerful...
and yet, oddly enough,
so soothing and gentle.
They were all grieving,
for ones who were injured & lost
for whatever reason,
it was just so trivial why one died.

I saw all sorts of people,
women who were crying,
men who extended the brotherly expressions
of manly embraces.
The mood was a strange sort of beautiful,
like a rainbow standing out amongst
the grieving animals,
trees,
flowers,
and grasses---
who had lost their own
during the preceding storm.

And each one of them
carried a candle...
each with a light,
that to me
represented a memory
of their fallen friends.
They spoke well of their friends.
They spoke well of each other.
They spoke of peace and togetherness.

And it began to rain...
Even though the rain extinguised their candles,
they each carried the light
that was shining for their loved ones
within their afflicting hearts
and grief-drunken minds.
And I remember
watching a candle
fall through the rain-cluttered air
to the ground...
And the tear that fell from my eye
for those I did not know
or know too well.
So I stretched my wings
and began to fly again.

---Franchot

I Dream of You of Me

Do you dream of me
as I do of you?
When you look in the mirror,
do my eyes stare lovingly back from the reflection?
Or when you laugh, do you hear my chuckle
matching yours?
Do you feel my touch when you hug yourself?
Or when you cry, do you feel my tears
tracing down your cheek?
And my arms wrapped around your precious body
to comfort all of your pains away?
Do you, my love
dream of me as I do you?

Do you feel the gentle, sweet caresses of my fingertips
along your back and neck
when you are tired and aching?
Or do you hear me singing softly
and ever so gently
in your ear, as I used to,
when our song
gently places your sleepy, cradling form
in the awaiting arms of the sandman?
Does a phrase on the radio
or something that somebody says
remind you of something that I used to say,
and bring me forth from the pristine drifts,
afloat on the currents of memories
in the back of your mind
to your tender arms?
Does a shirt
or a blanket

or a jacket
or a favorite place bring me back?
Tell me,
do you dream of me, my dearest, as I dream of you?

I hope so
because my heart won't let me forget you.
Neither will my memories,
nor lips,
nor empty embraces.
After all, you aren't here to fill them up.
And you always come back to my mind
on the delicate breeze of a passing thought
and the dear, candied kisses
of a loving memory.
Do you dream of me, my precious, as I dream of you?

---Franchot

Inmate

I sit...
and I really don't understand
why I'm here.
I look around me
and all I see are cold, brick walls
each covered with the memories
of you & I.
For moments that are each eternities all on their own
my heart and I sit staring at each other
for hours...days...months...
helplessly trapped in our little cell,
prisoners,
chained to loving you.

The years have gone by,
and I have watched, without understanding,
as my heart stands at the front window,
placing a candle on the pane
keeping watch for your returning home.
My tender heart,
she stands, forever looking out of that window
hoping to see you return.
Hoping to get a glimpse of you,
a sign that you still exist,
a sign that you still care,
that you still love us.

No matter what I do,
no matter how hard I try,
I can't get you outta my system.
You invade my thoughts,
you haunt my dreams,
you constantly hurt my heart...

I don't hear from you.
I probably don't even exist in your world
...anymore.
I have probably been replaced
and don't matter to you.
Yet, I still continue to care about you...

And as time rolls on
throughout our infinite sentence,
my heart and I still continue to sit
in that tiny cell,
forever prisoner
to loving you.

---Franchot

Still Waters

Still waters—
run silently, run deeply
like memories in time.
They, like those fond visions
that move you and soothe you,
are kinda "reach out and touch" retrospect
in an elegant design.

I went to those still waters
and looked over the edge to see
a fond memory
of both you and me—
together forever
was the way we would be,
but now by the still waters
the we is just me.

I looked and I saw us
in a tight embrace
the look of love and contentment
throughout your eyes and face
when you looked my way
and my heart began to sing
you kissed my lips
and caused my ears to ring.
It was a warm memory,
but only a daydream...

Still waters...
they run silent, they run deep
transforming the past into the present
so that the soul may reap
both the good and the bad,

the happy and the sad,
memories long gone
of love you have lost
and battles you've won.

I remember our fights
and the things that were said,
the harshness of my words
and your looks of utter dread.
Your verbal daggers,
that each cut worse than a knife
and the smooth making up aftermath
to set everything right.

I remember the embarrassment,
the pain, the long nights
...me taking extended walks
in an effort to take flight,
from you,
from the world,
and even myself
I had to leave
so that I could try
and get some help
from my Father in heaven
is where I turned
through prayer and patience,
the lessons that I learned
were allowance and the turning of the cheek,
but being with you was too much,
you were killing me.
So I ran away...

Now that I am alone,
I sit by those still waters
To remember the seeds to my life
that long ago were sewn:

those corners of my mind.
To see, to feel, to touch
those fond memories
the ones of you and me
at the time
when we was we,
instead of now,
where we is me--
by those still waters...

---Franchot

Printed in the United States
69570LVS00006B/700-741

9 781425 927745